Brynteg £10.49

Science and Technology
Medical Technology

Ann Fullick

www.raintreepublishers.co.uk
Visit our website to find out
more information about
Raintree books.

To order:
☎ Phone 0845 6044371
🖷 Fax +44 (0) 1865 312263
🖳 Email myorders@raintreepublishers.co.uk

Customers from outside the UK please telephone +44 1865 312262

Raintree is an imprint of Capstone Global Library Limited,
a company incorporated in England and Wales having
its registered office at 7 Pilgrim Street, London, EC4V 6LB
– Registered company number: 6695582

Text © Capstone Global Library Limited 2012
First published in hardback in 2012
The moral rights of the proprietor have been asserted.

Edited by Andrew Farrow, Adam Miller, and Diyan Leake
Designed by Victoria Allen
Original illustrations © Capstone Global Library Ltd 2011
Illustrated by Oxford Designers and Illustrators
Picture research by Elizabeth Alexander
Originated by Capstone Global Library Ltd
Printed and bound in China by CTPS

ISBN 978 1 406 22841 0 (hardback)
15 14 13 12 11
10 9 8 7 6 5 4 3 2 1

British Library Cataloguing in Publication Data
Fullick, Ann.
  Science and technology: medical technology. -- (Sci-hi)
  610.2'8-dc22
A full catalogue record for this book is available from the
British Library.

Acknowledgements
The author and publishers are grateful to the following
for permission to reproduce copyright material:
Alamy pp. **4** (© Mike Hill), **5** (© Medical-on-Line), **8**
(© wonderlandstock), **11** (© Spencer Grant), **13** (© Ace
Stock Limited), **25** (© doc-stock), **34** (© Melba Photo
Agency; Corbis pp. **19** (© Howard Sochurek), **21** (© Ian
Hooton/Science Photo Library), **22** (© Andrew Winning/
Reuters), **28** (© Dung Vo Trung), **31** (© Alexandra Beier/
Reuters), **32** (© Li Ga/Xinhua Press; Getty Images pp. **6**
(SSPL), **7** (Hulton Archive), **15** (Gallo Images - Media24),
23, **33** (Brandi Simons), **36** (Tim Hale/Workbook Stock),
37 (Alvis Upitis/Brand X Pictures); Science Photo
Library pp. **9** (Moredun Animal Health Ltd), **26** (Pascal
Goetgheluck), **29** (AJ Photo/HOP American), **30** (BSIP
LECA), **35** (John McLean), **40** (Geoff Tompkinson);
Shutterstock **contents page** top (© R. Perreault),
contents page bottom (© Andrea Danti), pp. **10**
(© Skyhawk), **12** (© Jason Stitt), **14** (© Condor 36), **20**
(© Alexonline), **27** (© R. Perreault), **39** (© Andrea Danti),
all background and design features.

Main cover photograph of a bionic hand reproduced
with permission of Alamy (© Steve Lindridge); inset cover
photograph reproduced with permission of shutterstock
(© Matt Ragen).

The publisher would like to thank literary consultant
Nancy Harris and content consultant Suzy Gazlay for
their assistance in the preparation of this book.

Contents

What is medical technology? 4

Some early medical technology 6

Diagnosing disease 8

Medicines 12

Surgery 14

Hearts, surgery, and technology 18

Life support 24

Lasers and ultrasound 26

Replacement surgery 30

Technology at the start of life 34

Nanotechnology and genetic technology 38

Timeline 42

Glossary 44

Find out more 46

Index 48

How can tattoos be removed?
Turn to page 27 to find out!

What is a nanobot?
Read page 39 to find out!

Some words are shown in bold, **like this**. These words are explained in the glossary. You will find important information and definitions underlined, <u>like this</u>.

WHAT IS MEDICAL TECHNOLOGY?

Doctors use all kinds of things to help make people better. A simple plaster can cover a small cut. A beam of light called a **laser** can be used to improve sight. A **life-support machine** can keep a body going for a few days whilst someone recovers from serious illness or **surgery**. All of these are examples of medical technology.

Looking inside the body

Doctors often need to be able to see inside our bodies to find out what is wrong with us. Lots of medical technology is used to help them. X-rays are good at showing up broken bones. MRI scans and CAT (CT) scans can show doctors any problems with the softer organs of our bodies, such as the liver or lungs.

This MRI scan shows the brain inside a skull.

Keeping you alive

If you are very ill, doctors use all sorts of medical technology to keep you alive. There are machines which can breathe for you and pump the blood around your body. There are ways of giving you food when you can't eat. Another machine can take waste materials out of your blood so they don't poison you. The machines which take over everything are life-support machines.

It takes a lot of technology to keep a seriously ill person alive.

In 2008, almost 14 million people went into hospital in the United Kingdom and about 38 million in the United States. Almost every patient will have needed something to help get them better, from a bandage to a life-support machine. That's a lot of medical technology.

SOME EARLY MEDICAL TECHNOLOGY

People have been using technology to try and cure diseases for thousands of years. Some early medical technology was quite frightening – and it often didn't work very well.

During prehistoric times, people didn't have hospitals but they did try brain surgery.

PREHISTORIC TIMES: BRAIN SURGERY

Scientists have found some prehistoric skulls with holes cut in them, known as **trepanning**. We know the patients survived, because bone had started to grow back over the holes. Scientists think prehistoric people were trying to cure fits and headaches in this way. They may have thought it would let evil spirits out of the skull.

THE 1600s: EARLY SURGERY

For hundreds of years, surgery was only done when it was the last chance to save a life. There was no way of putting people to sleep or preventing them from feeling pain other than giving them an alcoholic drink. Most people who lived through the pain of surgery died of infection (bacteria entering the wound) later. The best **surgeons** could take off a leg in a few minutes.

Early surgeons had to work quickly while the patient was held down. There were no painkillers in the 1750s, when this diagram was drawn.

THE 1800s: MAKING CHILDBIRTH SAFER

In the past, many women died through problems giving birth. Forceps had been invented in the 1600s but they were not in wide use until the 1800s. Forceps are tools which can help deliver a baby safely if it gets stuck during birth. They have saved the lives of thousands of mothers and babies.

THE 1900s: THE STETHOSCOPE

The stethoscope was invented in 1816. The tubes on a stethoscope allow doctors to listen to the sound of your heart beating. Doctors can hear air moving in and out of your lungs when you breathe, and it helps them to detect many different diseases. A stethoscope is a simple bit of medical technology which has saved many lives.

1800s

1900s

DIAGNOSING DISEASE

If you are ill, your doctor needs to find out what is wrong with you to be able to treat you. A good doctor will listen to you to find out what is wrong. Doctors will also use different types of medical technology to help them make a diagnosis (identify what exactly is wrong).

Testing the blood

Blood tests have been an important method of detecting disease for many years. Scientists create special **cells** which make **monoclonal antibodies**. Cells are the very small parts that form all living things. Monoclonal antibodies are special substances which target cells or chemicals in your body. They let doctors detect problems before they make you really ill.

Pregnancy tests use monoclonal antibodies to find out if a woman is pregnant as soon as possible. Then she can get good medical care. The bars in this test shows that the woman is pregnant.

Pregnant

Not Pregnant

Using monoclonal antibodies

Monoclonal antibodies are used in many tests for cancer. They can be used to screen people who show no signs of disease. Monoclonal antibodies can be used to find out which **micro-organism** (tiny living thing) is causing an infection. This is important because treating cancer early gives you the best chance of getting better. This means doctors can use the right medicine to make you better.

Looking at cells

Microscopes are another important piece of medical technology. They can magnify very small objects hundreds of times. Using microscopes, doctors can see the changes in cells when cancers grow. They can also identify the different **bacteria** that cause infections so they use the right medicine. Bacteria are very tiny living organisms that can cause disease.

Microscopes show doctors when cancer cells (shown here) are growing. Often a tiny sample of body tissue is taken to be checked for cancer cells under a microscope. **Electron microscopes** can magnify cells many thousands of times. They can be used to identify what is causing an infectious disease.

Looking inside your body

To diagnose what is wrong with you, doctors often need to be able to see inside your body without cutting you open. Medical technology makes this possible.

X-rays and CT scanners

Doctors have used X-rays for over 100 years but they are still the quickest way of seeing a broken bone. X-rays are created by using a special type of light. The light passes through the soft parts of your body but is stopped by hard tissue like bones and teeth, so it is just these that show up in a photograph. We call the special photograph that shows these bones an X-ray.

CT, or CAT, scanners use X-rays and computers to make lots of images of slices through your body. These pictures are very clear. Computers put all the information together to make a complete 3-D image of your insides. Doctors can use these images to diagnose many problems, from brain **tumours** (cancer lumps) to heart disease.

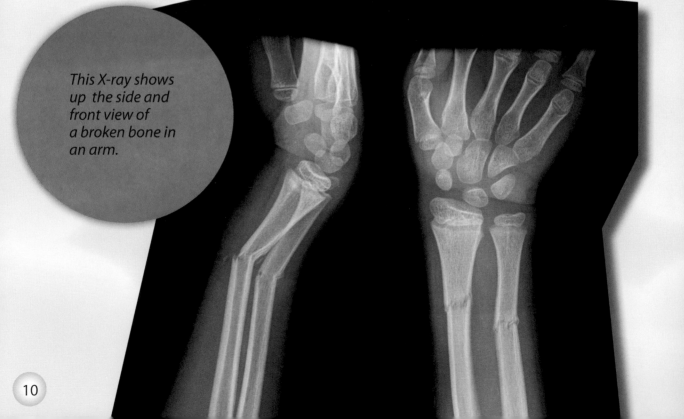

This X-ray shows up the side and front view of a broken bone in an arm.

WHO DID THAT?
X-RAYS

X-rays were first discovered in 1895 by Wilhelm Röntgen when he was investigating vacuum tubes. He called them X-rays because he didn't know what they were.

MORE WAYS OF SEEING INSIDE YOU

• Doctors also use ultrasound. This is sound that is too high for humans to hear. Ultrasound can go through the body.

• MRI scans give a detailed picture of the inside of your body. They are very safe to use. MRI scans are used to help doctors diagnose many different diseases.

• Endoscopes are tiny cameras which can be put inside your body. They can be used to help identify problems within the body. They can even be used to perform surgery.

• PET imaging lets doctors find very small areas of cancer. It is also good for seeing inside your brain.

A CT scanner is a big machine with a tunnel in the middle. The patient lies on a table which slides in and out of this tunnel. It doesn't take many minutes to get images of your whole body.

MEDICINES

Medicines can be used to make you better. They can make you feel more comfortable even if they cannot cure you. They protect you from disease. <u>Doctors also use vaccines (often through injections) to "teach" your body how to attack bacteria and viruses</u>. Often you can simply swallow a medicine in pill form. Some medicines need special technology to get inside your body.

Asthma attack

Asthma is a common problem in children and adults. In an asthma attack, the lining of the tubes which carry air down into your lungs swells up. The muscles around the tubes tighten and the airways become smaller. This makes it difficult to get air in and out of your lungs. It is important to get medicine into the lungs fast to relax the muscles and reduce the swelling, and help you breathe.

Medicine for the lungs

Asthma medicine is delivered using an inhaler which goes in your mouth. It gives a spray of reliever medicine which you breathe down into your lungs. Nebulizers make a medicine mist which you then breathe in through a mask.

Inhalers are used to give medicines to relieve asthma symptoms. They can also be used daily to give medicine which makes asthma attacks less likely.

Injecting medicine

Some medicines need to be given straight into your blood or your muscles. This is often done by injections, pumps, or drips. Some people have an illness called diabetes. Their body is unable to make the chemical insulin. Insulin is needed to help your cells get the sugar from your blood.

Some people with diabetes (called diabetics) need to inject themselves with insulin several times a day. A new way of treating diabetes is with an insulin pump which puts insulin under the skin all the time. More and more people are using these pumps.

This insulin pump puts insulin into your blood 24 hours a day. Many people with diabetes now use these pumps instead of injections.

SURGERY

During surgery, doctors go inside the human body to cure diseases or mend things that are not working well. As medical technology gets better, surgeons can carry out more and more amazing operations.

A chemical sleep

Modern surgery relies on **anaesthesia** (the loss of the sensation of touch through drugs). **Anaesthetics** make sure you can feel no pain during surgery. **General anaesthetics** put you into a deep sleep. Modern anaesthetics are very safe. They can be injected into your blood or breathed in. Machines check your heart beat, blood pressure, and breathing while you are in this deep chemical sleep.

Open surgery

A surgeon has to cut through the body wall to get to the organs inside. Much of the technology in the operating theatre is there to make the operation as safe as possible. There are special lights so the surgeon can see well. There are many different instruments to make it as easy as possible for the surgeon to work. They stop the bleeding and reduce the shock to the body.

For many operations, surgeons still open up their patients using very sharp metal knives called scalpels and sew them back together using stitches.

Cutting and sticking

Surgeons don't just use scalpels (sharp knives) any more. Lasers and even tiny, high-pressure jets of water can be used to cut parts of the body. Stitches are still often used in surgery. But more and more surgeons use special glues to bind tissue together as there is less bleeding and people heal faster.

In keyhole surgery, surgeons watch what they are doing on a screen. They control the instruments from outside the body.

KEYHOLE SURGERY

More and more operations are done using laparoscopic surgery (known as keyhole surgery). The surgeon puts a tube containing a tiny camera in through the tummy button. The instruments needed go in through one or two more tiny holes which are made. There is no big scar to heal. Most patients recover very quickly from keyhole surgery.

Robotic surgery

In some hospitals, robots carry out surgery under the control of a surgeon. This robotic surgery is becoming more common. Robots can make very tiny stitches and they never have shaky hands!

Detailed surgery

The robots used can carry out quite difficult and complicated surgery. The movements of a robot surgeon can be very carefully controlled. Doctors hope they will make surgery on areas like the eye, the ear, and the brain much easier and safer in future.

Surgery at a distance

Robotic surgery has made other things possible. In 2001 a woman in Strasbourg, France had an operation by keyhole surgery. The surgeons who did the operation were in the United States. This was almost 6,500 kilometres (4,000 miles) away. The robot surgeon which carried out the operation in France was controlled by an American and a French surgeon through computer links to the operating theatre. Many more distant operations have been done since. It means surgeons with special skills can help patients all over the world.

WHO DID THAT?
ROBOTIC SURGERY

One of the main scientists behind robotic surgery is Professor Brian Davies from the UK. In 1988 he developed the first robot ever to take tissue from a human patient. His best known robot is used in knee surgery.

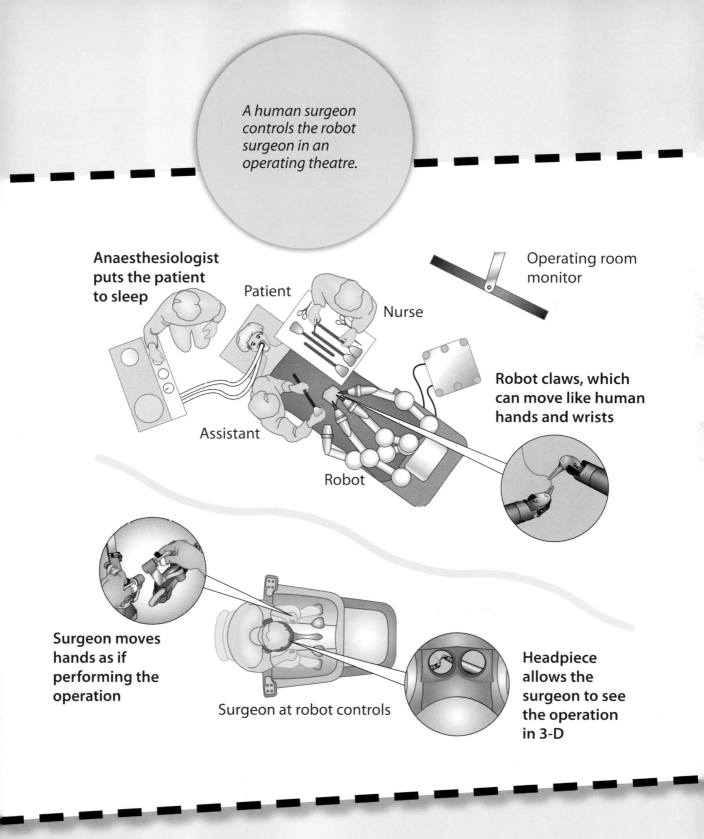

A human surgeon controls the robot surgeon in an operating theatre.

Operating room monitor

Anaesthesiologist puts the patient to sleep

Patient

Nurse

Robot claws, which can move like human hands and wrists

Assistant

Robot

Surgeon moves hands as if performing the operation

Surgeon at robot controls

Headpiece allows the surgeon to see the operation in 3-D

Hearts, surgery, and technology

Heart disease causes more deaths than any other disease in countries like the United States and the United Kingdom. However, some amazing surgery and clever technology mean that doctors now have more ways of helping patients with heart disease than ever before.

The human heart

The human heart is a bag of muscle. It pumps the blood to your lungs to pick up oxygen and then it pumps it around your body. Your heart beats around 60–70 times a minute all through your life. It has parts called valves. Valves are like doors which stop the blood flowing in the wrong direction. The heart muscle gets a good supply of food and oxygen from the coronary **arteries** (tubes or vessels).

These common problems can all stop the heart working properly.

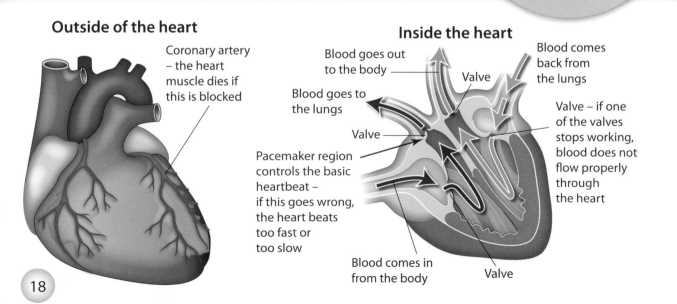

Outside of the heart

Coronary artery – the heart muscle dies if this is blocked

Inside the heart

Blood goes out to the body

Blood comes back from the lungs

Valve

Blood goes to the lungs

Valve – if one of the valves stops working, blood does not flow properly through the heart

Valve

Pacemaker region controls the basic heartbeat – if this goes wrong, the heart beats too fast or too slow

Blood comes in from the body

Valve

Heart problems

Lots of things can go wrong with your heart. If the coronary arteries get narrow or blocked, the heart muscle doesn't get the food and oxygen it needs. That can cause a heart attack. If the valves don't work properly, or the rhythm of the heart goes wrong, blood isn't pumped around your body properly.

Looking into the heart

If you start to get breathless when you climb the stairs, or get chest pains when you exercise, your doctor will want to check your heart. There is more than one way to look at the heart.

• An **ultrasound scan** (see page 28) can show doctors if the valves of the heart are working properly.

• A CT (or CAT) scan can show more detail of the size of the parts of the heart, and if the blood vessels are fine.

• In an **angiogram**, a special liquid which shows up on X-rays is injected into the blood. Then the heart is X-rayed and the coronary arteries can be seen.

HEART FACTS

Heart attacks are very common and are one of the leading causes of death in England. Each year in England, an estimated 111,000 people have a heart attack.

This angiogram shows healthy coronary arteries. This patient doesn't need surgery.

Bypass surgery and stents

For years doctors replaced narrow or blocked coronary arteries with bits of veins from other parts of the body. This is called bypass surgery. It is still used but is expensive and needs a general anaesthetic.

Today doctors often use **stents** to open up the blood vessels so the blood can flow again. A stent is a metal mesh which is placed in the artery. The artery takes blood carrying food and oxygen to different parts of your body. A tiny balloon is inflated to open up the blood vessel and the stent at the same time. Doctors can put a stent in place without a general anaesthetic. Many stents also release drugs. The drugs stop the blood from clotting (thickening) and blocking up the artery.

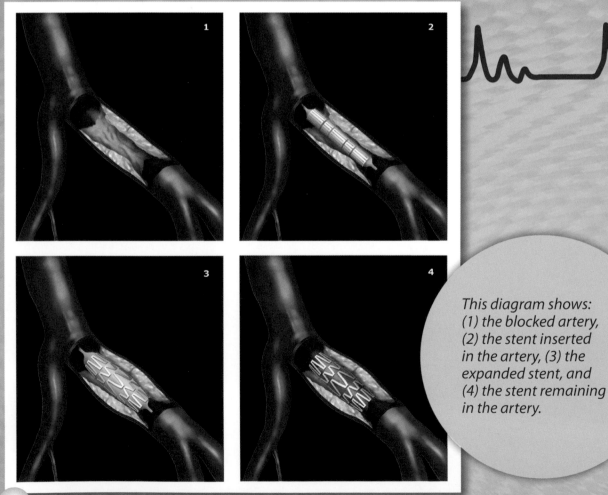

This diagram shows: (1) the blocked artery, (2) the stent inserted in the artery, (3) the expanded stent, and (4) the stent remaining in the artery.

Controlling the heart rate

If your heart beats much too slowly or very fast all the time, you can feel ill. A pacemaker can be implanted under your skin, with wires going into your heart. The pacemaker gives your heart a regular tiny electric shock so it beats at the right rate.

Replacing heart valves

Valves are the parts of the heart that control the flow of the blood. If they start leaking, they need to be replaced through open heart surgery. Doctors cut through the breast bone and pull the ribs apart to insert a new valve into the heart. The valve may be an artificial one made from plastic and metal. It may be a valve from an animal such as a pig or a cow.

BRIGHT IDEA

If someone has a heart attack, their heart stops beating. A controlled electric shock can start the heart beating again. Defibrillators are machines that do this. They are used in hospitals, but they are also found in shopping centres, restaurants, and sports stadiums. This has helped save many lives.

Defibrillators use an electric shock to restart a heart that has stopped.

Heart transplants

Sometimes a heart is so badly damaged or diseased that doctors cannot make it better. Then the only way to save the life of a patient is to give them a heart transplant. The new heart comes from a person who wished to give their organs to help someone else after they died (an organ donor). It needs to be inserted into the new patient as quickly as possible.

Connecting the heart

The new heart needs to be kept cool in special chemicals so it is healthy and undamaged. It may travel hundreds or thousands of kilometres in a box from one hospital to another. The damaged heart of the patient is stopped and removed. Then the new heart is put in its place.

Hannah Clark is a British girl who was given a heart transplant when she was a toddler. Her own heart was also left in place. Ten years later, the transplant was removed when Hannah's heart recovered!

Helping hearts

There are never enough donor hearts to go round. Scientists and doctors are trying to develop artificial hearts instead. LVADs (Left Ventricular Assist Devices) can help the heart to beat until it recovers and can work on its own. LVADs can also keep a diseased heart working for long enough for a donor organ to be found.

WHO DID THAT? HEART TRANSPLANT

The first heart transplant was carried out by Dr Christiaan Barnard in South Africa in 1967. The patient was Louis Washkansky and the donor was 23-year-old Denise Darvall, who had died in a car accident. Louis lived for only 18 days with his new heart but this was a medical breakthrough.

Artificial hearts

Some complete artificial hearts have been used to try and keep patients alive long enough to find an organ to transplant. There have been some successes but many problems with these hearts. In 2011 a team of French scientists will begin trials of a true artificial heart. They hope it will replace a diseased heart without the need for a transplant. An American team is also close to developing a permanent artificial heart to try out on patients.

This was the first artificial heart designed to completely replace a human heart. The patient lived for 151 days after he received it.

LIFE SUPPORT

The cells of your body need a supply of food and oxygen all the time. The waste made by your cells is poisonous so you need to get it out of your body. But during major surgery on the heart, or if you are seriously ill, your body can't keep going. This is when medical technology takes over. A life-support machine can keep you alive.

This diagram shows the processes involved when a person is on a life-support machine.

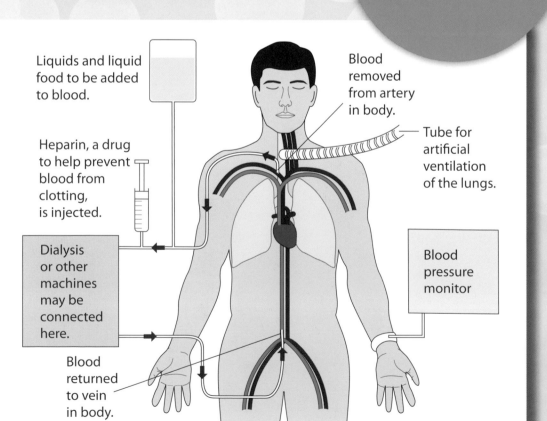

Liquids and liquid food to be added to blood.

Heparin, a drug to help prevent blood from clotting, is injected.

Dialysis or other machines may be connected here.

Blood returned to vein in body.

Blood removed from artery in body.

Tube for artificial ventilation of the lungs.

Blood pressure monitor

Life support

Different life-support machines do different jobs according to what the patient needs. The machines can take over the job of the heart and the lungs. They can take blood out of the body and put oxygen into the blood. They also remove the waste gas carbon dioxide. They then pump the blood back into the body. The machine checks the temperature of the blood and the levels of oxygen and carbon dioxide all the time. Early life-support machines were called heart–lung machines.

Kidney machines

A full life-support machine has a kidney dialysis machine joined on to it. This takes over the job of the kidneys. It cleans the blood by taking out waste. It also balances the levels of salt and water in the blood.

If your kidneys don't work you need to use a kidney dialysis machine several times a week to keep you alive and well.

LASERS AND ULTRASOUND

Laser light is a beam of very bright light that contains lots of energy (power). Doctors are finding new ways of using laser technology in medicine. Ultrasound scans use sound waves to see inside your body.

Lasers and eye surgery

The light energy in a laser is all focused on a very tiny area. This makes it very hot and very precise (accurate). Lasers are ideal for cutting and sealing wounds.

Being short sighted means a person can see close up but not far away, and being long sighted is the opposite. The shape of the eyeball causes these conditions. In eye surgery, doctors may use lasers to take very thin layers from the eye to correct the shape. After laser surgery, a person would not need glasses or contact lenses any more.

Using a laser to remove a tiny amount of tissue from the surface of your eye can give you perfect vision.

Scars and tattoos

Because lasers cut away very thin layers of tissue, they can be used in plastic surgery to help remove scars and birthmarks.

Lasers and cancer

Surgeons are finding more ways to use lasers in surgery. Because lasers are so hot, they seal any blood vessels that they cut so laser surgery causes less bleeding. Lasers are very useful for removing cancer tumours and for destroying cancer cells. They can shrink tumours which cannot be treated in any other way, making patients more comfortable. Lasers can be used to reach tumours deep in your brain.

Lasers are the best way of removing tattoos that people have done and then regret. However, even lasers leave some scarring.

Ultrasound pictures

Ultrasound scans help doctors see inside a body. Ultrasound scans help doctors and parents watch as a baby develops. Ultrasound can show if there are one, two, or more babies. They can show if the baby's heart and the brain are growing normally. Modern ultrasound images can even be three-dimensional (3-D). The parents can see their baby's face before it is born. More importantly, doctors can see any problems as the baby develops and be ready to help when the baby is born.

Ultrasound and surgery

Surgeons can use ultrasound scans to build up a 3-D image of a problem before they operate. Sometimes doctors have to separate twins who are born joined together (known as conjoined twins). They need lots of 3-D ultrasound pictures to plan the surgery. HIFU (high-intensity focused ultrasound) can also be used in surgery. It rapidly heats and seals blood vessels to stop bleeding.

Ultrasound scans make pregnancy safer and help more women have healthy babies.

Emergency ultrasound

When soldiers are injured or there is a big disaster, people need to be treated very quickly. Doctors hope ultrasound scans and HIFU can be used in an emergency to save many lives.

Sound in action

Sometimes hard lumps can form in the kidney and bladder. These are called stones. They are very painful and must be removed. Now doctors often use sound instead of surgery. They can use ultrasound or normal sound to focus on the kidney or bladder stones. The stones shatter into tiny pieces. These then come out of the body in urine.

When sound is used to break up kidney stones, the patient stays awake all the time.

REPLACEMENT SURGERY

Sometimes people lose an organ or tissue from disease. Sometimes a limb, an organ, or the skin or blood is lost in an accident. Doctors and surgeons need to use many different types of medical technology to save these patients.

Blood donation

In any operation, the patient may bleed a lot. People can lose a lot of blood in accidents too. If you lose too much blood you will die. You can be given a **blood transfusion** (someone else's blood put inside your body). Blood donors give blood which is stored until it is needed. There are four different blood groups. If you need blood you must be given the right blood group. If not, your body defences will reject it and you could die.

This human skin was grown in a laboratory. It is to replace the skin of a burns victim.

Organ donation

Damaged or diseased organs such as hearts, lungs, kidneys, livers, and skin can be replaced by a transplant. In most cases, organs can only be donated when someone (a donor) has died. <u>There are never enough donor organs for all the people who need them</u>. The body defences of patients who get a new organ will try to reject and destroy it. These defences are called the immune system. The patients will have to take drugs for the rest of their life to stop this from happening.

MICROSURGERY

Surgeons can now operate looking through magnifying lenses or even through a microscope. This lets them repair tiny blood vessels and nerves. It is called microsurgery. The thread that surgeons use to make stitches in microsurgery is so thin it can't really be seen just with your eyes.

Replacement microsurgery can reattach hands and other limbs.

Replacing lost limbs

One important use of microsurgery is to reattach limbs and other body parts which are lost in accidents. If the blood vessels and nerves can be joined together again, the person may be able to use their lost hand, finger, or toe almost as if they had never been damaged.

Different ways of moving

If surgery is not an option, many people still manage to lead active lives using wheelchairs and relatively simple artificial limbs to move around. Some people with artificial limbs can move faster than people who have their own legs!

Jeff Skiba of the United States is a high-jumper who has an artificial leg. He holds a world record for jumping 2.11 metres.

Replacing lost faces

Some of the most amazing microsurgery has been achieved doing face transplants. Several people who had terrible injuries to their heads have been given a new face from dead donors. The patients can smile and show other feelings. The new face gives the patients a much better quality of life than before surgery.

Robotic limbs

Often lost limbs are so badly damaged they cannot be reattached. Modern artificial limbs can look very like the real thing. Computer technology means that soon artificial limbs may also be able to work as well as the real thing. Some new limbs are able to link to the nerves left in the end of the old limb. The new limb would then work the way the old one did.

Growing new organs

Scientists are working on growing new organs using special cells called **stem cells**. Stem cells can grow into almost any cell in the body. In 2010 scientists gave 11-year-old Ciaran Finn-Lynch a new trachea (windpipe) grown using his own stem cells. The new trachea is covered in Ciaran's own cells. His body defences will not try to destroy it. So he does not need to take drugs to stop his body rejecting his new windpipe.

With a robotic arm like this you can open and close your artificial hand just by the power of thought.

TECHNOLOGY AT THE START OF LIFE

Everyone thinks they will be able to have a baby when they want one. <u>But one in every six couples has problems getting pregnant</u>. They have **infertility** issues. Advances in medical technology can help solve many of these problems.

In vitro fertilization

One common way of treating infertility is to use in vitro fertilization (IVF, or fertilization outside the body). Eggs are collected from the mother and mixed with **sperm** from the father outside the body. They combine to form **embryos**. An embryo is a baby at its earliest stage of development. One or two healthy embryos are then put back into the mother's body to grow and develop.

If the sperm do not move about very well, doctors can inject one single sperm into an egg.

egg

needle

sperm injected by needle

Freezing the future

For many years doctors have been able to freeze sperm. Now they can freeze eggs and even embryos as well. This can help patients in many ways. For example, if a young person needs treatment for cancer, it could possibly make them infertile. A young man needing cancer treatment can freeze sperm so that he can have children when he is older. Women can save their eggs before cancer treatment.

Some women freeze their eggs so they can delay having a baby until they are older. Couples can save spare embryos made through IVF to have another child later on.

Inside the womb

The womb is the organ inside a woman's body where a baby develops. An embryo's development from a single cell is amazing. However, things can go wrong. If a mother and baby have very different blood groups (see page 30), the mother's body may try to destroy the baby growing inside her. Doctors can give the baby blood transfusions inside the womb to keep it alive until it is born. Most other operations on unborn babies are still very new and risky.

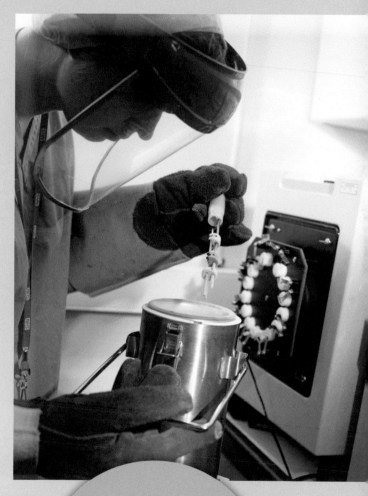

This technician is placing frozen human eggs in a container to transport them.

Twin success

Identical twins look exactly the same. They develop from a single fertilized egg. As they grow inside their mother, some can suffer from a condition called **TTTS**. This is where one twin gets more blood than the other. That twin becomes very big and the other very small. Often both babies die. Now, very successful surgery means doctors can change the blood vessels inside the womb, so both babies grow normally.

WHO DID THAT?

American surgeon Dr Ruben Quintero worked out how to change the blood vessels and save the lives of twins with TTTS.

Ten to fifteen per cent of identical twin pregnancies suffer from TTTS. The babies may need surgery before they are born to make sure they both grow well.

Shelt, Bess
40018457shelt   GA=12w0d   RAB 4-8L/OB   MI 1.1   Fetal Med
                                1.6/9.8cm/30Hz Tis 0.2   07/29/2009 03:14:50 PM
                                                              Routine
                                                              Har-mid
                                                              Pwr 100
                                                              Gn -1
                                                              C7 / M7
                                                              P3 / E3
                                                              SRI II 3

Born too soon

A normal pregnancy lasts for around 37–42 weeks. A baby born much earlier than this is called **premature**. Premature babies often have many problems because they are not fully formed. Their lungs don't work properly. They cannot control their body temperature. They can't suck milk so they can't feed. Without special help many of these babies die.

Incubators – an artificial womb

Incubators are special boxes which save the lives of many premature babies. They are placed over the baby's cot to keep it at the right temperature and supply it with extra oxygen. Incubators also check the baby's breathing and heart rate. Babies can be fed through tubes into their stomachs or even straight into their blood.

BRIGHT IDEA

Babies born before 30 weeks in the womb lack a special chemical called surfactant. This means their lungs can't stretch and fill with air easily. Scientists have developed ways of giving surfactant to them. This helps their lungs to work normally so they can survive.

It takes a lot of medical technology to save the life of a tiny premature baby.

NANOTECHNOLOGY AND GENETIC TECHNOLOGY

Some of the newest medical technology is happening at the level of molecules. <u>Nanotechnology works with material at the level of molecules</u>. This new technology uses very tiny particles which can only be seen with a special microscope called an electron microscope. <u>Scientists are using genetic technology when they look at the molecules which make up the genetic code</u>. This is the information in your cells which controls what you look like and how your body works.

Gold nanoparticles and cancer

Doctors are always looking for new ways of beating cancer. Cancer can grow in almost any area of the body. The chemicals used to treat cancer can often poison healthy cells as well. Gold nanoparticles are very small particles of gold. They are very useful. Gold doesn't react with other things in the body but it can be joined to chemicals which are attracted to cancer cells. They can also be attached to cancer-killing drugs. Then the gold nanoparticles carry the drugs straight into the tumour.

Gold nanoparticles and heat

Gold is a metal. It heats up very easily. Once the gold nanoparticles are in the cancer cells, they can be heated up using lasers. They get hot enough to kill the cancer cells. This means doctors need to use fewer costly drugs which can poison the body. Doctors hope using gold nanoparticles, drugs, and heat will become a very useful cancer treatment.

NANOBOTS AND NANOPROBES

In future, doctors hope they will be able to use tiny machines called nanoprobes to find different diseases in the body. Then they will send tiny robots the size of molecules, called nanobots, into the blood. They will carry medicine to the right place or destroy damaged cells and cancer.

Nanoprobes and nanobots might sound like science fiction. Gold nanoparticles will make them a reality.

In future, your doctor may look at your genetic code to help diagnose your diseases and give you the medicine that will work for you.

Genetic medicine

Your **genes** control what you look like and how your body works. Scientists have found genes for many different diseases. Some genes make you more likely to be ill. For example, some people have genes which mean they have a bigger risk of getting heart disease or cancer if they smoke. There are even genes which mean you have a high risk of getting breast cancer. Scientists have also found that our genes affect how well different medicines work for us.

Genetic engineering

Scientists can cut a gene from one living thing and add it to the genetic material of another. This is called **genetic engineering**. For example, tiny living things called bacteria can be given the gene for human insulin. The bacteria then make pure human insulin which is used to treat people with diabetes. Doctors and scientists also hope that one day soon, genetic engineering will be used to cure diseases caused by genes.

ENGINEERING A CURE

Some serious diseases such as cystic fibrosis and sickle cell disease are passed from parents to children through their genes. Cystic fibrosis affects the lungs and gut, and sickle cell disease affects the blood.

In future, with genetic engineering, we may be able to cut out healthy genes from the cells of a healthy person then insert them into the cells of a person with a genetic disease. This could keep them healthy for life.

Medical technology

Medical technology has come a long way. We can see deep inside the body using different types of scans. We can operate using scalpels, lasers, water, and ultrasound. We can replace damaged organs and limbs. We can operate through microscopes, using robots – even from one country to another.

The hospital of the future

Hospitals in the future may have no surgery – just nano-surgeons injected into our blood to heal us. Our genes may be engineered before we are born to remove the risk of many diseases. The medicine we are given will depend on our genes as well as our disease. No-one knows – but medical technology will try to keep us healthy for many years to come.

TIMELINE

10,000–6,000 BC (STONE AGE)	Trepanning, or simple brain surgery, is carried out without anaesthetic
1745	The Company of Surgeons, which later becomes the Royal College of Surgeons, is formed
1842	Dr Crawford Long uses the chemical ether as an anaesthetic for the first time
1867	Joseph Lister recommends using phenol (carbolic acid) as an antiseptic (totally clean substance) in operating theatres. This substantially reduces the death rate from infections.
1895	X-rays are discovered by the German scientist Wilhelm Röntgen
1896	X-rays are used in medicine to help set broken bones
1902	The first successful kidney transplant on a dog is carried out
1940s	Surgery to replace hip joints using artificial joints is developed
1940s	Heart pacemakers are developed
1953	The first heart–lung machine is developed by Dr John Gibbon
1954	The first successful human kidney transplant takes place in the United States, between identical twin brothers
1959	Scottish doctor Ian Donald and his team develop ultrasound to diagnose problems in unborn babies

1967	The first successful human heart transplant is carried out
1970s	CT scanners become widely used
1977	The first full body MRI image is published
1978	The birth of Louise Brown, the first baby to be conceived by IVF
1980	Lung surfactant is used on premature babies for the first time
1990	Keyhole surgery is now used on children
1991	The first robot surgeon operates on a person
1998	Stem cells from embryos are grown in a laboratory for the first time
2001	Keyhole surgery carried out on a woman in France is controlled by doctors in the United States
2002	The first heart operation is carried out on a developing baby in the womb
2005	The first partial face transplant is carried out in France using microsurgery
2010	A surgical team successfully transplant a windpipe grown from his own stem cells into a British boy

Glossary

anaesthesia loss of the sensation of touch or pain caused by drugs before surgery

anaesthetic chemical which causes the loss of sensation of touch or pain during surgery

angiogram way of seeing the blood vessels of the heart by injecting a special liquid which shows up on X-rays

artery blood vessel carrying blood away from the heart. The blood usually contains lots of oxygen.

bacteria micro-organisms which can cause disease

blood transfusion giving blood from one person to another

cell one of the very small parts that form all living things

electron microscope instrument which uses a stream of electrons to view things which are too small to be seen using a light. Electron microscopes magnify objects thousands of times.

embryo living thing in its earliest stages of development

gene unit of heredity which controls a feature or part of a feature about you. For example, there is a gene which controls whether you have dimples or not.

general anaesthetic anaesthetic that involves being put to sleep

genetic engineering process in which the genetic material of a cell is altered by replacing damaged genes or adding extra genetic material

infertility inability to produce offspring (babies)

laser beam of very bright light that contains lots of energy

life-support machine machine which takes over functions of your body

micro-organism very tiny organism that can only be seen using a microscope

microsurgery surgery on very tiny blood vessels and nerves. The surgeon performs the surgery looking through magnifying lenses or a microscope.

monoclonal antibody special substance which targets cells or chemicals in the body

premature born early. A premature baby is born after less than 37–38 weeks in the womb.

sperm male sex cells that join with an egg to form an embryo which may grow into a baby

stem cells cells which can grow into almost any other specialized type of cell in the body

stent metal mesh which is placed in a blocked artery to open it up and allow the blood to flow through

surfactant fluid in the lungs which keeps them open and expanded

surgeon doctor who performs operations

surgery opening up the body to remove parts that have a problem or mend damaged tissue

trepanning early way of trying to cure fits and headaches by making holes in the skull

TTTS (twin-to-twin transfusion syndrome) problem which can happen in identical twin pregnancies. One baby may receive more blood than the other. It becomes very big while the other stays very small.

tumour lump of cancer cells

ultrasound sound that is too high for humans to hear

ultrasound scan way of producing pictures of organs inside the body using ultrasound

virus micro-organism which causes disease and is infectious

Find out more

Books

Brain Surgery for Beginners (Human Body), S. Parker & D. West (Book House, 2010). A fun, extensively illustrated book on the body and common surgery – not just on your brain!

Frontiers of Surgery (Science at the Edge), Ann Fullick (Heinemann Library, 2004). Explore the amazing technology used in surgery of every kind, from an octopus which can stop part of your heart beating while doctors operate on it to the robot surgeons that doctors can use from another country.

Heart Man: Vivien Thomas, African-American heart surgery pioneer (Genius at Work!), E. Brit Wyckoff (Enslow Elementary, 2007). This book tells the story of the great African-American pioneer of heart surgery, which includes the impact of medical technology on this branch of medicine.

In Vitro Fertilization (Science at the Edge), Ann Fullick (Heinemann Library, 2002). This book looks at the medical technology needed to overcome infertility and help couples have a much-wanted baby.

Organ Transplantation (Science at the Edge), Ann Fullick (Heinemann Library, 2009). This book explores the exciting medical technology which allows doctors to replace body parts, from bits of the eye to the heart and lungs.

Programmes and websites

BBC Blood and guts: A history of surgery

This BBC series takes you through the history of surgery from its early, brutal beginnings through to the amazing and ever-changing medical technology used by surgeons today.